Farm Machines At Work

Plows

By Hal Rogers

The Child's World® Inc.

Published by The Child's World®, Inc.

Copyright © 2001 by The Child's World®, Inc.
All rights reserved. No part of this book may be
reproduced or utilized in any form or by any means
without written permission from the publisher.
Printed in the United States of America.

Design and Production:
The Creative Spark, San Juan Capistrano, CA

Photos: © 1999 David M. Budd Photography

Library of Congress Cataloging-in-Publication Data

Rogers, Hal, 1966-
     Plows / by Hal Rogers.
          p. cm.
     Summary: Describes the parts of plows, how they work, and what they do.
     ISBN 1-56766-755-4 (lib. bdg. : alk. paper)
     1. Plows—Juvenile literature. [1. Plows. 2. Agricultural machinery.] I. Title.

     S683 .R56 2000
     631.5'1--dc21
                                                                    99-089469

Contents

On the Job

On the job, a plow gets **soil** ready for planting. It chops up the soil and turns it over. The fields have been empty all winter. Sun, rain, snow, and frost can make the soil very hard. Farmers plow their fields every spring. Sometimes they plow in the fall, too.

The plow travels back and forth across the field. It loosens up the soil. Now the farmer can plant seeds to grow **crops.** Can you tell where the plow has been?

This plow has two sets of **blades.** There are six blades on the top, and six more on the bottom.

As the plow moves through the field, the

blades are dragged across the soil.

The blades cut into the soil and

turn it over.

A big **tractor** pulls the plow. A tractor must be powerful to pull such a heavy machine.

Now the tractor is at the end of a row.

It is time to turn around.

The plow must move over all of the soil in the same direction. If the farmer turns the plow around, it will move the soil in the opposite way. What does the farmer do? He has **controls** inside the tractor. The controls flip the plow upside down. Up and over goes the plow!

Climb Aboard!

Do you want to see where the farmer sits?

The field is very dusty. The farmer sits inside

the **cab.** It protects the farmer from dust.

The farmer uses a steering wheel to drive

the tractor. The farmer uses controls to run

the plow.

19

Up Close

The inside

1. The controls

2. The steering wheel

3. The driver's seat

The outside

1. The blades

2. The cab

3. The tractor

Glossary

blades (BLAYDZ)
Blades are sharp metal tools that are used to cut something. A plow uses blades to chop up and turn over soil.

cab (KAB)
A cab is where a farmer sits to drive a tractor. A cab has a seat, a steering wheel, and controls.

controls (kun-TROLZ)
Controls are tools that are used to help make something work. A farmer uses controls to make a plow work.

crops (KROPZ)
Crops are plants that are grown to produce food. Farmers grow crops to feed their animals or to sell to markets.

soil (SOYL)
Soil is the dirt in a field or a garden. A plow gets soil ready for planting.

tractor (TRAK-ter)
A tractor is a powerful machine that can move across fields and pull things behind it. Tractors can pull plows.